P9-CAL-237

P9-CAL-237

ABC

The Wild West
Buffalo Bill Historical Center
Cody, Wyoming

Florence Cassen Mayers

Harry N. Abrams, Inc.
Publishers
New York

For my children, Lela and Dara

Editor: Harriet Whelchel
Designer: Florence Cassen Mayers

Photograph credits:
Devendra Shrikhande: X, Y
Robert Weiglein: Title page, A, B, C, F, G (below), H (above), I (above and below left), J, L,
N, O, P, S (above and below), T (below), V (above)

Library of Congress Cataloging-in-Publication Data
Mayers, Florence Cassen.
ABC, the Wild West: Buffalo Bill Historical Center, Cody, Wyoming/Florence Cassen
Mayers.
        p.   cm.—(ABC series)
Summary: Presents in alphabetical order western art and memorabilia drawn from the
collections of the Buffalo Bill Historical Center.
ISBN 0–8109–1903–6
1. Frontier and pioneer life—West (U.S.)—Juvenile literature. 2. West (U.S.)—History—
Juvenile literature. 3. English language—Alphabet—Juvenile literature. 4. Buffalo Bill
Historical Center. [1. Frontier and pioneer life—West (U.S.) 2. West (U.S.)—History.
3. Museums. 4. Alphabet.] I. Buffalo Bill Historical Center. II. Title. III. Series: Mayers,
Florence Cassen. ABC series.
F596.M37 1990
978—dc20   90–440
                                                                                            CIP
                                                                                            AC

Published in 1990 by Harry N. Abrams, Incorporated, New York
A Times Mirror Company

Other Books in the ABC Series
ABC: Museum of Fine Arts, Boston
ABC: The Museum of Modern Art, New York
ABC: The National Air and Space Museum
ABC: Egyptian Art from The Brooklyn Museum
ABC: Costume and Textiles from the Los Angeles County Museum
      of Art
ABC: Musical Instruments from The Metropolitan Museum of Art
ABC: National Museum of American History
ABC: The Alef-Bet Book, The Israel Museum, Jerusalem

Title page:
Rosa Bonheur (1822–99). *Colonel William F. Cody*. 1889. Oil on canvas, 18½ x 15¼". Given
in Memory of William R. Coe and Mai Rogers Coe

As a boy, William F. "Buffalo Bill" Cody witnessed wagons moving
westward, the gold rush at Pike's Peak, and the formation of the Pony
Express. As a man, he worked as a trapper, a hunter, and a civilian
scout during the Indian wars. In 1883 he formed his famous Wild
West show, with which he brought the adventure of the West to the
rest of the country, and the world. The French artist Bonheur painted
his portrait when Buffalo Bill brought his show to France.

Introduction

In this delightful new ABC book, each letter of the alphabet is illustrated with one or more objects from the collections of the Buffalo Bill Historical Center in Cody, Wyoming. Made up of four museums in one—the Buffalo Bill Museum, the Whitney Gallery of Western Art, the Plains Indian Museum, and the Cody Firearms Museum—and located in the heart of the American West, the Historical Center explores and celebrates the art and history of the region as they were influenced by the frontier experience.

The illustrations for this book, chosen from among the approximately 150,000 objects in the Historical Center's collections, help to tell the story of the West and its people. History *is* the story of people. Whether they were famous individuals such as Buffalo Bill, Annie Oakley, and artist Charles Russell, or cowboys, Indians, and pioneers whose names have been lost to time, each contributed to the development of our understanding of the American frontier, and each is represented here.

For the youngest child, easily recognizable objects such as dolls, feathers, gloves, jugs, and vests provide a novel introduction to the alphabet. Older children, who will be intrigued by colorful moccasins and a bear-claw necklace, Buffalo Bill's saddle and a restored stagecoach from his Wild West show, handmade knives and cooking utensils, dramatic paintings of wild horses, hunters, and trappers, and much more, can use the book as a stepping-stone for further investigation. And readers of all ages will relish this unique keepsake of the Buffalo Bill Historical Center.

Joy L. Comstock, Director of Education
Buffalo Bill Historical Center

Above:
Gertrude Vanderbilt Whitney. *The Scout* (Buffalo Bill). c. 1922–24. Bronze, height 12′5″

This larger-than-life-size statue was made after Buffalo Bill's death in 1917. It was placed outdoors in a beautiful landscape setting in Cody, Wyoming. The artist, who purchased the land around the sculpture, later donated it to the Buffalo Bill Memorial Association, and it is where the Buffalo Bill Historical Center is located today.

Aa

Arrowheads

Prehistoric people did not have iron for weapons, so they made their weapons sharp with stone points. These stone points, called arrowheads, are often very attractive and when properly studied can tell a story about the creative people who made them long ago.

Projectile Points. Prehistoric. Flint and various stones; longest point: length 3″, width ¾″

Bb

Buffalo

Settlers and Indians alike hunted the buffalo for meat and hides. The huge animals, which once had roamed the plains in large numbers, became harder and harder to find in the wild. This artist, who was from New York City, found the model for his buffalo at the Bronx Zoo.

Henry Merwin Shrady (1871–1922). *Buffalo*. 1900. Bronze, height 12¼″

Cc

Cowboy

The cowboy pictured here is trying to catch a horse in order to saddle it. The artist described the scene he had painted: "In the corral the horses surged from one side to the other, crowding and crushing within the small rope circle. Above the sea of round, shiny backs, the thin loops swirled and shot into volumes of dust, the men wound in and out of the restless mass, their keen eyes always following the chosen mounts."

N. C. Wyeth (1882–1945). *Above the Sea of Round, Shiny Backs the Thin Loops Swirled and Shot into Volumes of Dust (R-G Colorado)*. 1904. Oil on canvas, 38¼ x 26″.
Gift of Mr. John M. Schiff

Dd

Doll

This doll's dress, with its elaborate beadwork and decoration, is similar to what a young Sioux woman would have worn for a special occasion.

Female Doll. Sioux tribe, c. 1885. Leather, paint, human hair, porcupine quills, snail shell, and turkey feather; height 15¼"

Ee

Entertainer

Annie Oakley's skill as a markswoman came to the attention of Buffalo Bill, who hired her for his Wild West show. Her sharpshooting act soon became one of the show's most popular atttractions.

Miss Annie Oakley, The Peerless Lady Wing-Shot. c. 1890. Four-color lithographic poster, 28½ x 19″. Gift of The Coe Foundation

Ff

Feathers

The owner of this beautiful warbonnet wore it so that all would know of his bravery and his success in battle.

Warbonnet and Trailer. Sioux tribe, Northern Plains, c. 1890. Deer hide, seed beads, eagle feathers, ermine, feather plumes, otter, horsehair, porcupine quills, paint, and ribbon; bonnet height 21½″, trailer 69 x 19½″

Gg

Gloves

A gauntlet is a special type of glove that covers the wrist and is worn to protect the hands from rough work. These decorative gloves probably were worn by an Indian man when dressed in his finest or while dancing at a powwow.

Gauntlets. 1920. Native tanned deerskin with bead decoration; length 15¼″, width 8⁷⁄₁₆″

Geysers

Geysers happen when water deep beneath the earth's surface
becomes so hot that it suddenly boils, causing water and steam to
spurt through the earth's crust straight up into the air. The artist who
captured these geysers was born in Germany but spent much of his
life exploring and painting the West.

Albert Bierstadt (1830–1902). *Geysers in Yellowstone*. c. 1881. Oil on canvas, 26¼ x 36".
Gift of Townsend B. Martin

Hh

Horses

Artist George Catlin traveled thousands of miles during several journeys in his goal to document the unspoiled West. In this painting he used strong, lively outlines to convey the energy, strength, and constant motion of the horses.

George Catlin (1796–1872). *Wild Horses at Play*. c. 1855–70. Oil on paper board, 18 x 25″. Gift of Paul Mellon

Hunters

Like many other artists of his day, Frederic Remington lived in the East but was fascinated by the West. He became famous for his paintings and sculptures of western scenes. Every year he traveled west to gather ideas for his art, making sketches along the way. The final works were created in his New York and Connecticut studios.

Frederic Remington (1861–1909). *The Buffalo Hunt*. Oil on canvas, 34 x 49″.
Gift of William E. Weiss

Ii

Henry F. Farny (1847–1916). *Days of Long Ago*. 1903. Oil on paper mounted on board, 37½ x 23¾″

John Mix Stanley (1814–72). *Last of Their Race*. 1857. Oil on canvas, 43 x 60″

Indians

As the population of the United States grew, American Indians of the Plains tribes faced many changes: there was less open land on which to roam and there were fewer wild animals to hunt. Many artists made paintings in order to tell people about these changes. Some painted the quiet beauty of an earlier time, others showed the sadness as that time was ending, and still others made portraits of individuals. They wanted to remember the traditions and nobility of a group of people who had to adjust to a new way of life.

Joseph Henry Sharp (1859–1953). *White Swan—Crow*. c. 1903. Oil on canvas, 17⅝ x 11¾″

Jj

Jug

Much of the West is desert, and it was important for the western traveler always to carry water. This water jug was made from a carved-out gourd. Its owner was Mexican, and the battle scenes decorating the outside suggest that he may have been a soldier.

Gourd Canteen. 1886. Hand-painted gourd with leather strap, height 10″.
Gift of The Coe Foundation

Kk

Knife

In the West knives were used for many purposes, from cutting meat to carving wood. This hunting knife was probably made by its owner.

Hunting Knife. c. 1880. Handmade curved steel blade with straight bard guard, bone handle with metal butt; blade length 6½″, handle length 4⅞″

Ll

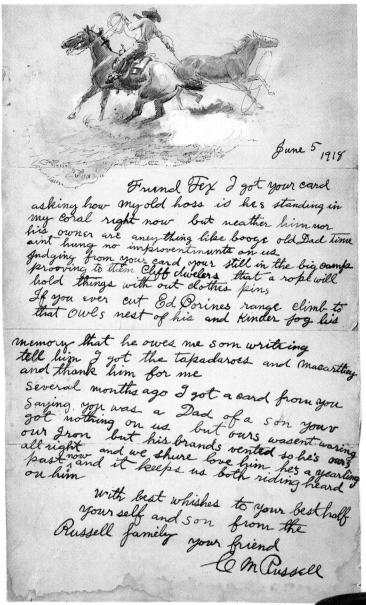

June 5 1918

Friend Tex I got your card asking how my old hoss is he's standing in my coral right now but neather him nor his owner are aneything like booge old Dad Time aint hung no improventmunts on us judging from your card your still in the big camp prooving to them Cliff dwelers that a rope will hold things with out clothes pins

If you ever cut Ed Borines range climb to that Owls nest of his and kinder jog his memory that he owes me som writing tell him I got the tapadaroes and macarthey and thank him for me

Several months ago I got a card from you saying you was a Dad of a son your got nothing on us but ours wasent waring our iron but his brands vented so he's ours all right now and we shure love him hes a yearling past and it keeps us both riding heard on him

with best whishes to your best half your self and son from the Russell family
your friend
C M Russell

Letter

The artist Charles Russell captured scenes of the West, even in his letters. In this note Russell, who had an adopted son, shared his friend's happiness at having a new baby boy. (Look for one of Russell's paintings on the O page.)

The moccasin shoe we wear today is a plainer variation of the decorated soft-leather version worn by the Indians.

Charles M. Russell (1864–1926). *Friend Tex.* 1918. Watercolor and ink on paper, 14½ x 7⅝″. Gift of William E. Weiss

Moccasins. Hidatsa tribe, c. 1900. Deerskin, porcupine quills, seed beads; length 10³⁄₁₆″, width 4⅛″. Dr. William and Anna Petzoldt. Gift of Genevieve Petzoldt Fitzgerald

Mm

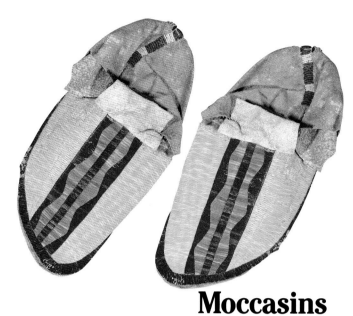

Moccasins

Moose

The moose is the largest member of the deer family. It can grow to be as tall as eight feet at the shoulder.

Alexander P. Proctor (1862–1950). *Moose*. Modeled 1893, cast c. 1907. Bronze, height 19½″

Nn

Necklace

The Indians valued animals not only as sources of food and clothing but also for the special qualities that each animal possessed. The bear represented a creature that was half man, half beast, with great spiritual as well as physical strength. The otter was prized for its soft, beautiful fur.

Bear-Claw Necklace and Trailer. Mesquakie tribe, c. 1840–50. Grizzly-bear claws and otter fur with ribbons, glass beads, and multicolored bead medallions; necklace length 12″, inside diameter 6½″, trailer length 60″. Adolph Spohr Collection. Gift of Mr. Larry Sheerin

Outlaw

The Royal Northwest Mounted Police kept order in the Canadian West. The artist explained the scene this way: "Two Royal Northwest Mounted Police have arrested a pair of horse thieves and are disarming them. In all countries this is the first thing done by officers of the law. No prisoner is considered safe while wearing a weapon."

Charles M. Russell (1864–1926). *When Law Dulls the Edge of Chance.* 1915. Oil on canvas, 29½ x 47½". Gift of William E. Weiss

Pp

Pioneer

Although stories of western life often seem to focus on the deeds of men, this portrait illustration for the cover of a book about a young pioneer who traveled the Oregon Trail serves as a reminder of the many brave women who moved westward to explore the new frontier.

W. H. D. Koerner (1878–1938). *Madonna of the Prairie*. 1922. Oil on canvas, 37 x 28¾″

Qq

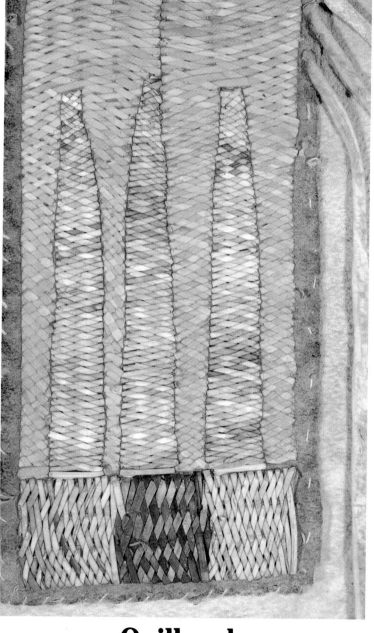

Quillwork

This special design was created by weaving together porcupine quills. The colors probably came from natural sources, such as berry juices.

Portion of a Man's Shirt. Hidatsa tribe, 1900. Dyed porcupine quills on leather; shirt length 30⅛", width 18⅛". Gift of Irving H. "Larry" Larom

Rr

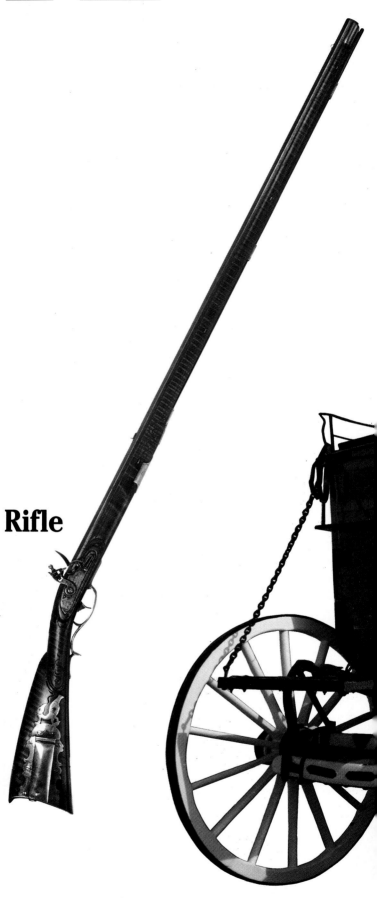

Rifle

This beautifully crafted rifle was used for hunting in the West.

Buffalo Bill used this saddle, which is decorated with his image and inscribed with his name, in his Wild West show.

Made by Nicholas Byer. Pennsylvania Rifle. 1790–1800. Bird's-eye maple with brass mounts, steel barrel and locks; length 58″

Honorable William F. Cody Saddle. 1893. Hand-tooled leather with embossed silver disk and silver inlay inscription; height to top of horn 45½″, seat length 15″, overall length 29⅜″. Museum Purchase from William Cody Boal

Ss

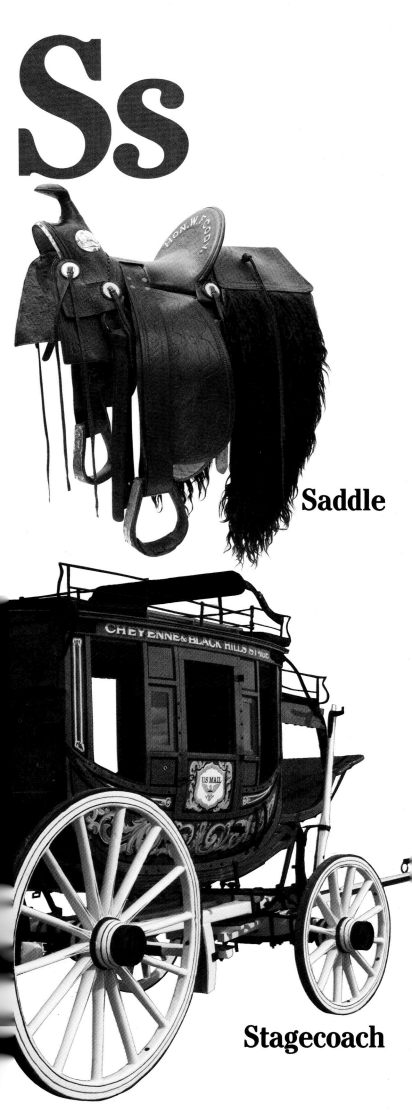

Saddle

Stagecoach

Before the completion of the railway system connecting East and West in the late nineteenth century, the horse-drawn stagecoach carried people and mail across the country. The stagecoach holdup was a popular part of the Wild West show.

Buffalo Bill's "Deadwood" Concord Stagecoach (restored). 1840. Molded wood with metal supports and leather interior. Lent by Mr. Glenn E. Nielson

Tt

Tepees

Trapper

These cone-shaped tents, made of animal skins drawn tightly around a frame of stout wooden poles, were home to the Indians of the Great Plains region.

Trappers made their living by capturing animals and selling their pelts. The artist probably painted this portrait of a trapper, known only as Louis, during a summer trip to the Rocky Mountains in 1837.

Joseph Henry Sharp (1859–1953). *Tepees on the Prairie*. 1902–10. Oil on canvas, 12⅛ x 17⅞″

Alfred Jacob Miller (1810–74). *Louis—Rocky Mountain Trapper*. c. 1837. Watercolor on paper, 7⅞ x 5¾″. Gift of The Coe Foundation

Uu

Utensils

Each of these hand-forged iron utensils was made with a long handle and hook at the end for hanging by a brick fireplace oven.

Utensils (*clockwise from below left*): Strainer Ladle. c. 1890. Length 18½″, diameter of ladle 5½″. Three-Pronged Fork. c. 1860. Length 13¾″. Ladle with Side Pourer. c. 1860. Length 14″, diameter of ladle 2½″. Two-Pronged Cooking Fork. Length 14½″. Spatula. c. 1860. Length 18¼″

Vv

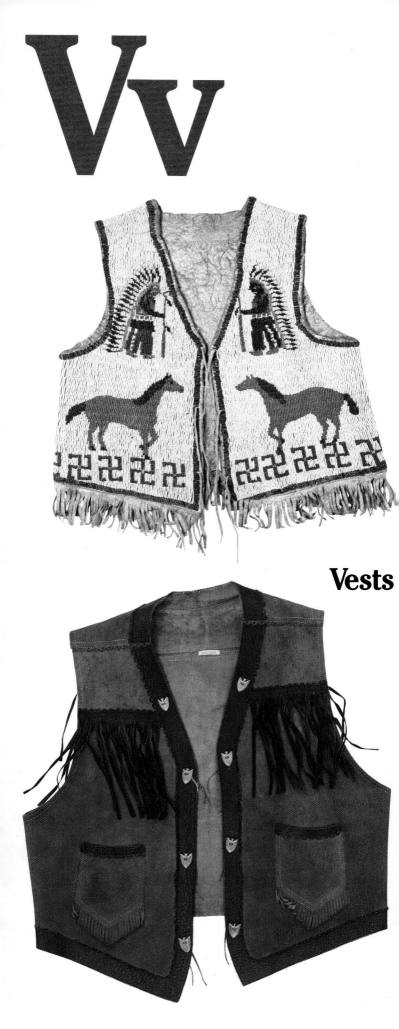

Vests

A young Sioux boy once wore this colorful vest (*above*). The swastika designs forming the bottom border had no specific meaning and were used for decoration only. The brown suede vest (*below*), which is decorated with specially worked leather along its edges, would have been worn by a cowboy.

Boy's Vest. Sioux tribe, South Dakota, 1885. Deerskin beaded in lazy stitch; length with fringe 16⅞″, width 16⅝″

Man's Vest. c. 1935. Suede outside, smooth leather inside, black grained leather trim with scalloped and pierced inner edge; back length 18⅝″

Ww

Waterfall

John Henry Twachtman was known as an Impressionist artist. He did not care to show every detail of a scene, as a photograph would. He wanted to show how a scene looked at a certain time and in a certain light. He saw that the bright, clear daylight appeared to bounce off the rushing waterfall so that the water and everything around it almost seemed to dissolve, and he put that lovely, misty quality in his painting.

John Henry Twachtman (1853–1902). *Waterfall in Yellowstone*. c. 1895. Oil on canvas, 23⅜ x 16½". Gift of Mr. and Mrs. Cornelius Vanderbilt Whitney

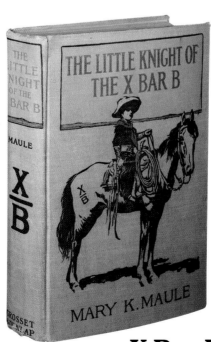

X Bar B brand

Because animals often wandered far from home in search of food, ranchers marked their livestock with a special symbol, or brand, so they could pick out their animals from all the others. The ranches were often called by the name created by the letters of their brand, as in the X Bar B ranch referred to in the title of this book.

Mary K. Maule. *Little Knight of the X Bar B.* 1910. Grossett and Dunlap Publishers, New York. Formerly in the Collection of William Cody Bradford

Yy

Yellowstone

As the West continued to be developed, the government decided to make sure that the extraordinary natural wonders of the region would be preserved for future generations. In 1872 almost 3500 square miles of land were set aside to form Yellowstone National Park, filled with dramatic geysers, flowing waterfalls, and deep canyons.

Thomas Moran (1837–1926). *The Golden Gate*. 1893. Oil on canvas, 36¼ x 50¼″

Zz

Zigzag

A zigzag is a series of short, sharp angles that create a particular pattern. This zigzag pattern was woven into a bag in which household utensils were kept.

Corn-Husk Bag. Nez-Perce tribe, 1905. Woven Indian hemp with corn-husk decorations and rawhide thong trim, 18¼ x 13⅜″